UNBREAKABLE SPORTS RECORDS?

GYMNASTICS RECORDS THAT WILL BE TOUGH TO BEAT

Kerry Kelaher Fredeen

Mitchell Lane PUBLISHERS

Mitchell Lane

PUBLISHERS

mitchelllanepub.com

2001 SW 31st Avenue
Hallandale, FL 33009

First Edition, 2026.
Author: Kerry Kelaher Fredeen
Designer: Ed Morgan
Editor: Tammy Gagne

Series: Unbreakable Sports Records?
Title: Gymnastics Records That Will Be Tough to Beat

Library bound ISBN: 979-8-89260-725-4
eBook ISBN: 979-8-89260-730-8

Photo credits: cover, p. 9, 13, 15, 17, 23, 25, 31, 33, 35, 45, 49, 51, 55, 56 Alamy; p. 4-5 freepik.com; p. 7, 27, 37, 43 wikimedia; p. 18, 41, 53 Shutterstock

CONTENTS

INTRODUCTION

It's a 10!

It was September 23, 1988. The Women's All-Around Gymnastics final had come down to its final competitors at the Summer Olympics in Seoul, South Korea. And the competition was as close as it could be.

The Soviet Union's Elena Shushunova was locked in a tight battle with Romania's Daniela Silivas for the All-Around medal. The two athletes had to perform in all four disciplines: floor exercise, balance beam, uneven bars, and vault.

Shushunova had the lead going into the finals. But then Silivas pulled ahead. Both athletes received high scores. They even got a few perfect 10s. That was the highest score given in gymnastics at the time. Silivas had a slight lead as the pair went into the last event.

The final event was the vault. Silivas scored a 9.9. Shushunova needed a score of 9.975 to tie for the gold medal. A 10 would give her the win.

Silivas led off the competition with a twisting Tsukahara vault. This move requires the athlete to complete a somersault with a twist. She felt confident that she had done well. The judges awarded her a score of 9.9.

Shushunova took her turn, doing the same Tsukahara vault. She was more controlled, and she flew further through the air than Silivas. The judges gave her a 10. She had won. At a press conference afterward, she said, “I can just say that I’m very happy.”

Sushunova
on the beam

The first perfect 10 had been awarded at the 1976 Olympics to Romania's Nadia Comăneci. Over the course of those games, she earned seven perfect scores, a total that hadn't been bested since. Both Shushunova and Silivas got seven 10s in Seoul in 1988, but neither could break Comăneci's record.

Gymnastics is an ancient sport. Both the events and the rules for competition have changed a lot over time. Records are **continually** toppled. But in the last several decades, some outstanding athletes have set records that seem impossible to break.

IT'S A 10!

Comăneci celebrates a perfect 10 and a gold medal at the Montreal Olympics in 1976.

CHAPTER ONE

Golden Girl Larisa Latynina

When Larisa Latynina was growing up in Ukraine, she dreamed of becoming a ballerina. Her family was poor, and dancing brought beauty into her life. But when her local dance studio closed, she turned to gymnastics as an outlet for her talents. Latynina used her dance background to add elegance to the sport. Her artistry would lead her on a golden path to a record that would be hard to break.

Latynina won many championships at the school level. She began competing for the Soviet National Team. During her first appearance at the World Championships in 1954, she placed a promising fourteenth in the All-Around.

In 1956, Latynina made her Olympic **debut** at the Summer Games in Melbourne, Australia. She was twenty-one years old. She was competing against Olympic veterans, such as Hungary's Ágnes Keleti, who had won gold in the 1952 Helsinki Games, and Czechoslovakia's Eva Bosáková, who took a bronze at those games. Despite the stiff competition, Latynina won gold medals in the All-Around, floor exercise, and vault. She also took home three additional medals as a member of the Soviet team: the gold in the All-Around, the silver in the uneven bars, and the bronze in team portable apparatus. This event only appeared in the Olympics in 1952 and 1956.

Latynina excelled in her first Olympic appearance.

At the 1960 Olympics in Rome, Italy, Latynina continued her winning ways. She repeated as an All-Around champion, and she scored another gold in floor exercise. In addition, she helped the Soviet team earn another All-Around gold. Scoring two more silvers, in uneven bars and balance beam, as well as a bronze in vault, her medal count soared to eleven. Seven of the tokens were gold.

Latynina's last Olympic appearance came in Tokyo, Japan, in 1964. She repeated her gold-medal performances in All-Around and floor exercise. She became the first female athlete to win nine gold medals in any sport. While her gold medal tally was tied by U.S. swimmer Katie Ledecky at the 2024 Paris Games, Latynina's nine golds is still a record among all gymnasts, male or female.

Whose Record Did Latynina Beat?

The start of WWII delayed Keleti's Olympic career.

Ágnes Keleti was a promising young gymnast. She was the Hungarian National Champion and had her eyes on competing in the Olympics. But her dreams were put on hold with the outbreak of World War II (1939-1945). Because they were Jewish, she and her family were forced into hiding, and Keleti was not able to compete until 1952 in Helsinki, Finland. This was where she won her first gold medal. She won an additional four golds at the Melbourne Games in 1956, competing against Latynina. Keleti's record of five golds stood until Latynina broke it in 1960.

Along with the golds, Latynina's two silvers and two bronzes in Tokyo made her the most decorated Olympic athlete ever, with eighteen total medals. This record would stand until 2012, when swimmer Michael Phelps broke it at the Olympics in London, England. Latynina was present when Phelps broke the record, and she joked with *The New York Times*, "Forty-eight years is almost enough time to hold a record."

Latynina was gymnastics' first international superstar. Bela Karolyi, who coached Olympic champion Nadia Comăneci, told *The New York Times*, "[Larisa] was our first legend . . . when she stepped out on the floor, all eyes were on her. She demanded attention and respect."

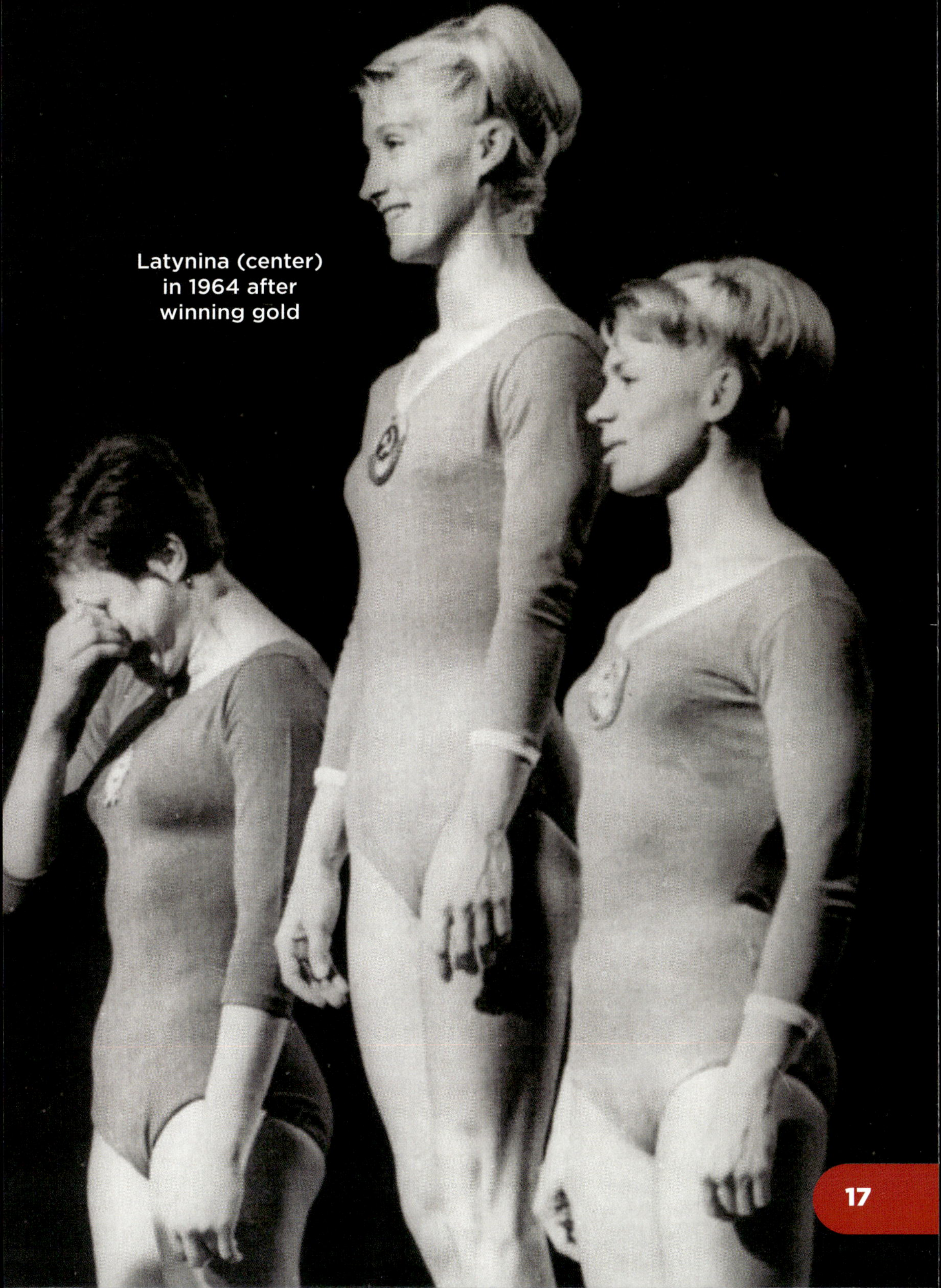

Latynina (center)
in 1964 after
winning gold

Biles could break Latynina's gold medal record in Los Angeles in 2028.

Chasing Latynina's Record

Simone Biles of the United States is considered by many to be the greatest gymnast of all time. She earned her seventh Olympic gold medal in the 2024 Paris Games. Only time will tell if she can beat Latynina's record. She could do it if she competes in the Los Angeles Olympics in 2028. Biles told a reporter from NBC, "Never say never. The next Olympics is at home, so you just never know."

CHAPTER TWO

Nadia Comăneci's PERFECTION

Nadia Comăneci was just six years old when she was discovered by Romanian gymnastics coach Bela Karolyi. He recognized her talent, even though she was so young. He told *Newsweek*, "The technical **purity** of her performance is her most brilliant characteristic." Comăneci won her first National Junior Championship in 1970. She won many competitions after that.

CHAPTER TWO

In 1976, Comăneci was part of the Romanian team at the 1976 Olympics in Montreal, Canada. Her first event was the uneven bars. Each athlete had to perform the same routine in the event. The judges saw something special in Comăneci's performance. Recalling the event, Comăneci told Olympics.com, "I added **amplitude** to every skill, so it looks like in the book, but I just added a little something. It was my personal touch." She performed flawlessly, and the judges rewarded the effort.

But when the score was posted, the scoreboard read "1.00." The scoreboards could only hold three digits. They weren't prepared for a score of 10.00.

A time-lapse photo of Comăneci on the uneven bars in Montreal in 1976

Comăneci was confused at first. It looked like a very low score, but she knew she'd done better than that. Finally, the judges clarified the score. She had been given the first perfect 10 in Olympic gymnastics.

She would go on to score six more 10s in the uneven bars and the balance beam. She won gold in the All-Around, balance beam, and uneven bars. And she took home a team silver for All-Around and a bronze in the individual floor exercise.

Comăneci was also the youngest gymnast to win an All-Around gold. She was just fourteen years old. That is a record that is highly likely to stand, since the participation age for female gymnasts was raised to sixteen for the 2000 Sydney Olympics to help protect the health of young athletes. Younger athletes' bones are not fully developed. Gymnastics can be tough on the human body, and working too hard, too soon can lead to career-ending injuries.

Séguin may have scored the first gymnastics perfect 10.

Was Comăneci Indeed the First?

Nadia Comăneci is widely considered to be the holder of the first perfect 10 in Olympic gymnastics. But there are people who say otherwise. In the 1924 Paris Olympics, a French gymnast named Albert Séguin scored a 10 for a required vaulting event that was later discontinued. In the same Olympic Games, more than twenty gymnasts received scores of 10 on the rope climb, an event that was scored but not artistically judged. Because Comăneci 's performance was scored in part for its artistic elements, many people see her 10 as the first true perfect score in gymnastics.

Comăneci was just fourteen years old when she went to her first Olympics. Years later, during an interview with the Olympics.com website, she said, “I was asked, ‘What do you think you’re going to do at the Olympics?’ I said, ‘I don’t know. I hope to win a medal and, hopefully, it’s gold”. She accomplished much more than that. She became a legend in gymnastics.

Daniela Silivas on the beam.

Chasing Comăneci's Record

It was always going to be difficult to top Comăneci's seven perfect 10s. The closest anyone has come was when both Elena Shushunova and Daniela Silivas tied the record in 1988. But in 2006, the International Gymnastics Federation changed its scoring system. A 10 is no longer a perfect score. The new Code of Points system, which considers difficulty and execution, has led to many higher scores, but none as celebrated as Comăneci's perfect 10.

CHAPTER THREE

Vitaly Scherbo's GOLDEN HAUL

Vitaly Scherbo got an early start in gymnastics. His mother enrolled him in classes in his native Belarus when he was seven years old. She hoped it would channel his wild energy.

CHAPTER THREE

Scherbo was a quick study. His coaches saw his potential and arranged for him to attend a state school for promising athletes. He quickly advanced and was named to the Soviet National Team at age fifteen. He won his first national championship in 1990 and placed second in the All-Around at the 1991 World Championships.

Scherbo's first Olympics was in Barcelona, Spain, in 1992. His coaches didn't see him as their best medal prospect. He was talented but **inconsistent**. Scherbo was about to prove them wrong.

Scherbo on the rings in Atlanta in 1996

He was competing for the Unified Team, which was formed after the breakup of the Soviet Union in 1991. In the first competition, he helped lead the team to gold in the Team All-Around. Two days later, he triumphed in the Men's Individual All-Around.

But Scherbo was just getting started. On August 2, he competed in four individual competitions. He earned near-perfect scores on the parallel bars, the rings, the vault, and the pommel horse. He won four gold medals on the same day.

Scherbo told *The New York Times*, "Obviously, I'm thrilled. I certainly didn't expect this to happen. It seemed to me it would be impossible to win so many gold medals."

Andrianov on the pommel horse in Montreal in 1976

Whose Record Did Scherbo Beat?

Before Scherbo began competing in gymnastics, another Soviet gymnast named Nikolai Andrianov won a then-record four gold medals in the sport at the 1976 Montreal Games. When Scherbo was a young gymnast, Andrianov was one of his coaches. "He was my **mentor**. He taught me how to concentrate, to keep myself inside myself," Scherbo told the Olympics.com website. Though Scherbo beat his mentor's record for single-game golds, Andrianov still holds the record for most overall medals for a male gymnast with fifteen.

CHAPTER THREE

At the young age of twenty, Scherbo did something no one had accomplished before. He was the first gymnast to earn six gold medals in gymnastics at a single Olympics. He was gearing up to compete in Atlanta, Georgia, in 1996, and was favored to take the All-Around gold again.

But Scherbo's gold streak was sidelined. His wife, Irina, was in a near-fatal car accident before the Atlanta Games, and he stopped his training to be by her side. *The New York Times* reported that as she recovered, Irina told him, "You are maybe the strongest gymnast mentally in the world, and you just spent four years working for another Olympics. It was very hard, and you must not stop right at the end."

Scherbo salutes the crowd in Atlanta.

Scherbo agreed to resume his training. While he didn't take gold in Atlanta, he did win four bronze medals. He retired after the Atlanta Games, telling *The Washington Post*, "Atlanta will be it for me. I want to retire while I'm still kicking butt, not when my butt is getting kicked."

He was later **inducted** into the International Gymnastics Hall of Fame. Scherbo and his wife went on to open the Vitaly Scherbo School of Gymnastics in Las Vegas, Nevada. They worked to help kids develop their athletic abilities, confidence, and self-esteem.

Shinnosuke's performance in the Paris 2024 games made him a gymnast to watch.

Chasing Scherbo's Record

Scherbo's record of six golds in a single Olympics has stood for more than thirty years. That's a long time for a record to stand. But Japan's Oka Shinnosuke could be the one to break it. His first Olympic appearance was at the 2024 Paris Games. He won four medals, including three golds. His surprising triumph in the Individual All-Around made him an athlete to watch in the future.

CHAPTER FOUR

Oksana Chusovitina's STAYING POWER

The Olympics happen every four years. Qualifying takes a lot of work and dedication. Many Olympic gymnasts only appear in one or two Olympic Games. It's rare for one of these athletes to make it to three.

Gymnastics is a physically demanding sport. Most gymnasts who go on to compete at the top levels begin their training at the age of five or six. By the time they make it to the Olympics, they have trained for thousands of hours. That training takes a great toll on an athlete, both physically and mentally.

CHAPTER FOUR

Most of the top female gymnasts reach their peak early. They tend to retire in their late teens or early twenties. That makes the achievements of Uzbekistan's Okasana Chusovitna even more inspiring.

Chusovitina's first Olympic appearance was at the Barcelona Games in 1992. This was the same year Vitaly Scherbo won his six gold medals. Like Scherbo, Chusovitina had been a high-energy child, and gymnastics was a way to focus that energy. Her skills helped her and the Unified Team win a Team All-Around gold in Barcelona.

Chusovitina competed in eight Olympic Games.

CHAPTER FOUR

In 1996, Chusovitina competed for her native Uzbekistan at the Atlanta Games. She also represented the Uzbekistan National Team in Sidney, Australia, in 2000 and in Athens, Greece, in 2004. She obtained German citizenship in time to represent that country in the 2008 Olympics in Beijing, China, where she won a silver medal in the vault event. It was the only medal for the German women's gymnastics team in Beijing. She competed under the German flag once more, at the 2012 London Games.

With six Olympics already under her belt, Chusovitina again represented Uzbekistan at the 2016 Olympics in Rio de Janeiro, Brazil. While she didn't medal, she was an inspiration to all the athletes and the fans. When she stepped up to compete, the announcer reminded the audience that her first Olympics appearance was "before most of us were born."

Olga Tass

Whose Record Did Chusovitina Beat?

Hungarian Olga Tass started gymnastics in 1941, but World War II delayed the beginning of her Olympic career. She couldn't compete until the 1948 London Games. Tass won six medals, including a team gold, over her Olympic career. Her record of four **consecutive** games stood until Chusovitina competed in Beijing in 2008.

Chusovitina competed for Uzbekistan again in the 2020 Tokyo Games. When she didn't make the finals in the vault, she announced her retirement. She told the International Gymnastics Federation, "It was really nice. I cried tears of happiness because so many people have supported me for a long time. I didn't look at the results, but I feel very proud and happy. I'm saying goodbye to sports." It looked like her eighth Olympics would be her last.

But always a competitor, Chusovitina decided to try for one last appearance. She kept training and had her sights set on Paris in 2024. An injury while training for a qualifying meet put an end to her chance of a ninth straight Olympics. There would indeed be no ninth appearance for the forty-eight-year-old athlete. But eight total Olympic appearances will be incredibly tough for another gymnast to beat.

Simone Biles

Chasing Chusovitina's Record

It's rare for a gymnast to appear in more than two Olympic games. Because the sport is so hard on the body, many gymnasts retire at a young age. Simone Biles was twenty-seven when she won gold at the 2024 Paris Games. That was her third Olympic appearance. To make it to nine consecutive Olympics, Biles would be fifty-one years old at the ninth appearance. This makes Chusovitina's record likely to stand.

CHAPTER FIVE

Simone Biles's World Championship MEDALS

Simone Biles had a challenging childhood. She and her younger sister spent time in foster care until they were adopted by their grandparents. She was an active and energetic child, always willing to take risks. In an interview with the Academy of Achievement, she described herself as "Just a very brave child."

Biles discovered gymnastics on a field trip to a gym with her day-care group at the age of six. When coaches saw her imitating the moves of older athletes, they told her family she should take gymnastics classes. She took to the sport right away. She quickly rose through the junior ranks and came in first at several national events.

CHAPTER FIVE

Biles began competing at the senior level in 2013. She won the All-Around title at her first World Championships in Antwerp, Belgium. She also won a gold in floor exercise, a silver in vault, and a bronze in balance beam. Her dominance of the World Championships had just begun.

Biles returned to the World Championships in 2014 where she won four more golds and one more silver. In 2015, she scored four golds and one bronze. Her next stop was the 2016 Rio de Janeiro Games.

Competing at her first Olympics, Biles led Team USA to the All-Around gold. She won the Individual All-Around gold medal. She also brought home two more golds and a bronze in other events.

Biles performs at the 2013 World Championships In Antwerp, Belgium.

Between Olympic cycles, Biles continued to perform extremely well at the World Championships. She took home four more golds in Doha, Qatar, in 2018, including the Individual All-Around. She also added one silver medal for the uneven bars and one bronze on balance beam.

But it was at the 2019 Championships in Stuttgart, Germany, where Biles cemented her reputation as the greatest of all time. With five gold medals, she reached a total of twenty-five medals overall—the most any gymnast had earned.

Scherbo's record of twenty-three world championships stood for twenty-three years.

Whose Record Did Biles Beat?

Vitaly Scherbo had already made gymnastics history in 1992 by winning six gold medals in one Olympics. He added to his legend when he won his twenty-third World Championship medal in 1996. It took twenty-three years for that record to be broken.

Biles hit a roadblock at the 2020 Tokyo Games. The games were delayed until 2021 due to the COVID-19 virus. These Olympic Games were played without **spectators**. Biles withdrew from the team All-Around final for mental health issues. She told reporters she realized, “It’s been really stressful, this Olympic Games. I think just as a whole, not having an audience, there are a lot of different **variables** going into it.” She returned after a break to compete on the balance beam, where she won the bronze.

Biles’s tough decision to step away from the All-Around was seen as a very brave move. Her teammate Jade Carey told CNN Sports, “When Simone withdrew from the team final at the Olympics, I saw pure strength. . . . It’s hard to take a step back and truly take care of yourself in our sport and that is what she showed the world.”

Biles at the Tokyo Olympics in 2021

At the 2023 World Championships, Biles added five more medals to her count, including an All-Around gold. By this time, she had won a total of thirty World Championship medals. She also became the most decorated gymnast of all time, with thirty-seven medals between the Olympics and the World Championships. After the Championships, Biles thanked her fans for their support on social media, saying "Your encouragement, love, and belief in me has been **instrumental** in my success and recovery. Knowing that you were there, cheering me on, gave me the strength to push through the toughest moments."

Gymnastics is an exciting sport. It continues to change over time. For all the records set, there are always going to be athletes who will strive to break them.

SIMONE BILES'S WORLD CHAMPIONSHIP MEDALS

Biles displays her World Championship gold medals in Stuttgart in 2019.

CHAPTER FIVE

Biles's friend and rival Rebeca Andrade could also be her successor.

Chasing Biles's Record

Many gymnastics fans see Rebeca Andrade as Simone Biles's biggest competitor. At the 2020 Tokyo Games, Andrade became the first female Brazilian gymnast to score an Olympic medal. Andrade and Biles have a rivalry, but the two athletes are friends. Biles told reporters at an Olympics press conference, "She's very close to me—I've never had an athlete so close." Andrade won gold over Biles in floor exercise at the 2024 Paris Games. The Brazilian gymnast has just nine world championship medals as of 2024, so she still has a way to go to beat Biles's total, but many people think she may be the one to watch.

Think FAST!

Test your new knowledge of gymnastics by answering the following questions.

1. **At which Olympics did Larisa Latynina make her debut?**
   - A. 1952 Helsinki Games
   - B. 1956 Melbourne Games
   - C. 1960 Rome Games

2. **Oksana Chusovitina and Vitaly Scherbo both competed for which team at the 1992 Summer Olympics?**
   - A. Germany
   - B. Unified Team
   - C. Uzbekistan

3. **How old was Nadia Comăneci at her first Olympics?**
   - A. Fourteen
   - B. Fifteen
   - C. Sixteen

4. **What gymnast holds the record for the most gold medals at a single Olympics?**
   - A. Nikolai Andrianov
   - B. Bela Karolyi
   - C. Vitaly Scherbo

5. **What made Simone Biles withdraw from part of the competition at the Tokyo Games?**
   - A. COVD-19
   - B. A leg injury
   - C. Her mental health

Answers: 1. B 2. B 3. A 4. C 5. C

Glossary

amplitude
The height or quality of a movement

consecutive
Directly following another instance

continually
Happening repeatedly

debut
The first performance of an athlete

inconsistent
Undependable in performance

inducted
Admitted into an organization

instrumental
Playing an important role in an accomplishment

mentor
An experienced advisor

purity
Having a clear and perfect quality

spectators
People who attend an event such as a gymnastics competition to watch it

variables
Details that may change, affecting an outcome

Find Out More

IN PRINT

Daniels, Rachel. *Meet Simone Biles*, Mitchell Lane Publishers, 2023.

Illustrated Sports Encyclopedia, DK, 2023.

Mooney, Carla. *Swimming Records That Will Be Tough to Beat*. Mitchell Lane Publishers, 2026.

ON THE INTERNET

***Olympic Games*, n.d.**
https://olympics.com/en.

***International Gymnastics Federation*, n.d.**
www.gymnastics.sport.

***USA Gymnastics*, n.d.**
https://usagym.org.

Index

About the Author

Kerry Kelaher Fredeen lives in Hollywood, California. She's written several books for young readers. When she's not busy writing, she works at a Southern California library. A lifelong sports fan, she fell in love with gymnastics watching Nadia Comăneci at the Montreal Olympics.